7 Enemies *of* Your **DESTINY**

GEORGE MFULA

7 Enemies of Your Destiny

Copyright © 2024 by George Mfula

ISBN: 978-0-6459774-1-7

Published by Faith Digest Library Media

All rights reserved. No part of this publication may be reproduced, stored in a retrieval system, or transmitted in any form or by any means, electronic, mechanical, photocopying, recording or otherwise, without the prior written permission of the copyright owner, with the exception of brief excerpts in magazines, articles, reviews, etc.

For further information or permission, please contact:

Rise And Walk Church Inc. Sydney Australia
Phone: +61. 425-338-781
Email: rawc-sydney@hotmail.com
Website: www.riseandwalk.org.au
Text design by: Sriraman Ramachandran
Cover design by: George Mfula
Interior design by: Sriraman Ramachandran

National Library of Australia Cataloguing - in - Publication Data:

Author: Mfula George –
Title: 7 Enemies of Your Destiny(pbk)
ISBN: 978-0-6459774-1-7
Subjects: Christian Living / Religious Book

Unless otherwise stated, all Scriptures are taken from the New King James Version (The Holy Bible, New King James Version) Copyright © 1982 by Thomas Nelson, Inc. Used by permission. All rights reserved.

Contents

Mandate v

Introduction 1

Chapter One
Fear 7

Chapter Two
Spiritual Ignorance 29

Chapter Three
Disobedience 47

Chapter Four
Unbelief 63

Chapter Five
Laziness 81

Chapter Six
Pride 99

Chapter Seven
Unrenewed Mind...119

Final Words of Faith...139

Mandate

God once said to me, "Go! I'm sending you like I sent Moses, my prophet to liberate my people from all oppressions of the devil through the preaching and teaching of the Word of Faith. Raise the foundations of many generations, prophesy over them and school them into supernatural knowledge, wisdom, and exploits; impart into them my power and wisdom; release them into their glorious and unparalleled destinies."

Introduction

Enemies of your destiny are things that have the potential to stop God's divine purpose for your life from coming to pass. Often, people are afraid of the enemies without and not the enemies within. The "enemies without" are also known as "the enemies outside." Things such as witches, powers of darkness, wicked spirits, and cosmic powers. Then the enemies within are things such as fear, ignorance, laziness, pride, unbelief, sin and much more. Many people, even Christians, spend their entire lives blaming the devil for their failures. Of course, he is our greatest enemy. However, Jesus overcame Him for us on the cross! Thus, instead of focusing on him, let's focus on Jesus!

Then, the other thing is that the enemies within can open a door to the enemies without. However, that can only happen if you allow it yourself through your spiritual ignorance or disobedience. I believe the devil without can't overcome you except you allow him through your disobedience to God's Word. Most of the people walk in defeat because of the enemies within. My prayer is that you will have a vigilant spirit in Christ Jesus to overcome all the enemies of your destiny. However, for that to happen, you will always need Bible faith or the spirit of faith at work in your life. Faith is non-negotiable—it is, in fact, a must!

Romans 8:28-31

And we know that all things work together for good to those who love God, to those who are the called according to *His* purpose. For whom He foreknew, He also predestined *to be* conformed to the image of His Son, that He might be the firstborn among many brethren. Moreover whom He predestined, these He also called; whom He called, these He also justified; and whom He justified, these He also glorified.

There is nothing the devil can do about your life and destiny in Christ Jesus. God has purposed in His heart to make your destiny enviable to your generation, regardless of your background. However, you need to learn how to walk in dominion over the enemies of your soul or destiny. Many people, even Christians, wonder why things are not moving or working for them. Yes, some of them spend considerable time in prayer and fasting. Well, you need to overcome your enemies within because they are the most dangerous.

For example, no matter how many prophecies you may receive from God concerning your destiny, fear can stop them from coming to pass. Hence, if you want to see your destiny succeed, then overcome the enemies of your destiny first, especially the ones within. For instance, harbouring unforgiveness in your heart will hinder your prayers from being answered. Certainly, unforgiveness is a sin and one of the topmost enemies of your destiny. That is why, no matter how much you pray, cry, or fast, it will always hinder your prayers. Just be careful!

Isaiah 59:1-2

Behold, the Lord's hand is not shortened,That it cannot save; Nor His ear heavy,That it cannot hear. But your iniquities have separated you from your God;And your sins have hidden His face from you, So that He will not hear.

May God give you dominion over all the enemies of your soul and destiny. You are here on Earth to fulfil your God-ordained destiny in Christ Jesus!!

CHAPTER ONE

FEAR

Deuteronomy 20:1-4

"When you go out to battle against your enemies, and see horses and chariots *and* people more numerous than you, do not be afraid of them; for the Lord your God *is* with you, who brought you up from the land of Egypt. So it shall be, when you are on the verge of battle, that the priest shall approach and speak to the people. And he shall say to them, 'Hear, O Israel: Today you are on the verge of battle with your enemies. Do not let your heart faint, do not be afraid, and do not tremble or be terrified because of them; for the Lord your God *is* He who goes with you, to fight for you against your enemies, to save you.'

The Mystery Behind Fear

Sometimes it sounds like fear is a small thing for it to be the enemy of our destinies. Besides, everyone can fear from time to time—so what is the matter? Why is fear such an issue when we talk of fulfilling our destinies in Christ Jesus? Well, fear is the opposite of faith, which means where fear is, faith is not. Then, where you find fear, you won't find God and the Holy Spirit. For you and me to operate in the spiritual realm of God's holy presence, we need faith and not fear. No one will ever fulfil their destiny operating in fear.

Nowadays, most of the communities are fear-driven, controlled, and manipulated. Of course, many people are living in fear of the economy. How did it all start? Well, the media has communicated most of the fear through their videos or news broadcasts. Thus, instead of your faith getting built, it is getting destroyed. Hence, when you are watching your television programs, you must carefully choose what to watch. During the COVID-19 era, I believe many people died because of fear communicated to them through the media. Fear is the number one enemy of our destiny, and we must never give it any place in our lives.

All fears in this wicked world have spiritual roots, and all of them culminate in the spirit of bondage. There are people today with great business plans or ideas who can't start one because of the fear of the unknown or failure. God forbid! People of God, fear is not the enemy outside! It is the enemy within your soul or spiritual system. Hence, before you can even talk of walking in victory over the devil and his cohorts afflicting your life, you must first deal with your fears within. When you allow fear in your life, just know that you have given the enemy of your destiny permission to triumph over you. Fear is a destiny killer!

Numbers 13:30-33

Then Caleb quieted the people before Moses, and said, "Let us go up at once and take possession, for we are well able to overcome it." But the men who had gone up with him said, "We are not able to go up against the people, for they *are* stronger than we." And they gave the children of Israel a bad report of the land which they had spied out, saying, "The land through which we have gone as spies *is* a land that devours its inhabitants, and all the people whom we saw in it *are* men of *great* stature. There we saw the giants (the descendants of Anak came from the giants); and we were like grasshoppers in our own sight, and so we were in their sight."

The number one reason many destinies have suffered at the hands of the devil is because of fear. There is no medical prescription for fear because fear is not a physical problem but a spiritual one. Hence, to deal with it from the roots, you and I need the power of God in Christ Jesus. The *beauty industries* today can make body lotions or shower gels for stress, but never for fear. Why? That is because fear is a spirit, and its source is the devil Himself. For example, Peter the Apostle walked on water, and as soon as fear entered him, he sank. The spirit of fear has sunk the destinies of many people, including their businesses and careers.

From my observation, the number one thing many people struggle with in life is the fear of death. That is why some people have health covers and others have personal medical doctors. Of course, there is nothing wrong with having medical doctors and health covers, but not at the expense of fear. Sadly, even Christians have no longer faith in divine healing or health. They believe more in the medical industry than they believe in God's power. Saints, I totally believe there is nothing wrong with having health insurance, but not because of fear. Just make sure it is not the spirit of fear driving you to get all these things.

Many years ago, I read a story about a popular pop star who wanted to live for 150 years. He had kept a team of 12 doctors who always stayed with him. Not only that, but he also used to sleep on an oxygen bed and did not forget to put on a mask and gloves before meeting anyone. Of course, you can hire doctors and have private health insurance, but not because of fear. He appointed 12 doctors at home who would daily examine him from hair to toenails. His food was always tested in the laboratory before serving it on his table. He also appointed 15 people to look after his daily exercise and workout.

Unfortunately, the man, no matter how much he invested in his health to live long, even 150 years, died young. Friends, you, and I can have doctors as much as we want, even out of fear, yet only God is the giver of life. Of course, there is nothing wrong with having doctors as they are God-sent. They help a lot with health concerns, however, to do it out of fear is not a good thing. Make sure whatever you do is not out of fear. Why? That is because fear is one of the greatest enemies of our glorious destinies in Christ Jesus.

Whenever you sense fear in your life, just know that there is something wrong with your faith. Anytime you tolerate fear for any apparent reason, the devil will take advantage of you. The Holy Spirit won't live or stay in an environment where fear gets accommodated. If you want the Holy Spirit to work with you, then eliminate fear from your life with His empowerment and help in Christ Jesus. If you allow fear in your life, God's holy presence will lift off your life. Remember what Jesus said when they reported to him that Jairus' daughter was dead? He counteracted the report of fear with faith. Fear can stop and kill your destiny if you wilfully or ignorantly allow it.

Mark 5:21-24

Now when Jesus had crossed over again by boat to the other side, a great multitude gathered to Him; and He was by the sea. And behold, one of the rulers of the synagogue came, Jairus by name. And when he saw Him, he fell at His feet and begged Him earnestly, saying, "My little daughter lies at the point of death. Come and lay Your hands on her, that she may be healed, and she will live." So *Jesus* went with him, and a great multitude followed Him and thronged Him.

Fear must never be your portion, even at the point of your lowest moments in life.

Mark 5:35-39

While He was still speaking, *some* came from the ruler of the synagogue's *house* who said, "Your daughter is dead. Why trouble the Teacher any further?" As soon as Jesus heard the word that was spoken, He said to the ruler of the synagogue, "Do not be afraid; only believe." And He permitted no one to follow Him except Peter, James, and John the brother of James. Then He came to the house of the ruler of the synagogue, and saw a tumult and those who wept and wailed loudly. When He came in, He said to them, "Why make this commotion and weep? The child is not dead, but sleeping."

Saints, when you examine the above Bible verse, why do you think Jesus immediately responded by saying: Don't be afraid; only believe? It was because He did not want to give room to the spirit of fear. In fact, people later ridiculed Him after putting them outside. Above all, it was all about faith—people did not have faith in Him, hence the weeping. Now, let us look at what happened to the dead girl after Jesus prayed for her in the house.

Mark 5:40-43

And they ridiculed Him. But when He had put them all outside, He took the father and the mother of the child, and those *who were* with Him, and entered where the child was lying. Then He took the child by the hand, and said to her, "Talitha, cumi," which is translated, "Little girl, I say to you, arise." Immediately the girl arose and walked, for she was twelve years *of age*. And they were overcome with great amazement. But He commanded them strictly that no one should know it, and said that *something* should be given her to eat.

Never tolerate fear in your life. It will corrupt your entire life and destiny in Christ Jesus!

Fear is the Devil's Stronghold

If you want to find out where the devil lives, just look at the lives of people or Christians who tolerate fear in their lives. When you are afraid of anything in life, the devil and his cohorts will always take you for granted. Without a doubt, fear is the devil's number one stronghold in our lives. Hence, no matter how long or hard you pray, fear will render your prayers in effective. There was a time in the Bible when the envoys from Assyria came to Judah to deliver the message of war to King Hezekiah. All they did was plant a seed of fear by the negative things they spoke to the king and people.

2 Chronicles 32: 16-19

Furthermore, his servants spoke against the Lord God and against His servant Hezekiah. He also wrote letters to revile the Lord God of Israel, and to speak against Him, saying, "As the gods of the nations of *other* lands have not delivered their people from my hand, so the God of Hezekiah will not deliver His people from my hand." Then they called out with a loud voice in Hebrew to the people of Jerusalem who *were* on the wall, to frighten them and trouble them, that they might take the city. And they spoke against the God of Jerusalem, as against the gods of the people of the earth–the work of men's hands.

Fear has always been the hiding place of the devil—it is his stronghold in every generation. The devil, who is also the enemy of our destinies, will always use fear. Why? That is because it is the quickest way to disconnect us from divine alignment with God. Many people, even Christians, have lost battles of life because fear stood in their way. If you want to see how weak and defeated the devil is, just eliminate fear from your life. Besides, no matter how much knowledge you may have in life when you are afraid of anything, life becomes tough and bitter. Hence, don't entertain fear even for a moment, no matter the case!

There was a time in Samaria when Elisha, the Prophet of God and his servant Gehazi, came under siege to the Syrian military. Saints, that occurrence generated fear in Gehazi such that he was almost a dead person. The man couldn't see God's divine protection around them. Hence, fear will always frustrate your spiritual sight or perception. God forbid! Beloved, each time the devil wants to paralyse your entire life and destiny, he will always use the spirit of fear. Now, let us look at what Elisha said to his servant, Gehazi.

2 Kings 6: 15-17

And when the servant of the man of God arose early and went out, there was an army, surrounding the city with horses and chariots. And his servant said to him, "Alas, my master! What shall we do?" So he answered, "Do not fear, for those who *are* with us *are* more than those who *are* with them." And Elisha prayed, and said, "Lord, I pray, open his eyes that he may see." Then the Lord opened the eyes of the young man, and he saw. And behold, the mountain *was* full of horses and chariots of fire all around Elisha.

Each time you give into fear, you have just lost your ground of victory. Many times, the reason people lose battles, even on the brink of victory, is giving up too early to fear. Fear can cripple your entire life, destiny, and generation if tolerated. Certain fears in some families are generational! No wonder no one has ever achieved anything, whether female or male. God forbid! I know of many people who used to be bound by the spirit of fear, but Jesus set them free by His power. Many years ago, I prayed for a woman who was bound by the spirit of the fear of death. She got deprived of sleep—she had never slept for a long time!

Hebrews 2:14-15

Inasmuch then as the children have partaken of flesh and blood, He Himself likewise shared in the same, that through death He might destroy him who had the power of death, that is, the devil, and release those who through fear of death were all their lifetime subject to bondage.

The above Scripture is what I used to pray for the woman who was bound by the spirit of the fear of death. Jesus Christ delivered her on the spot, and she became a free person. To Jesus be the glory!!

Breaking the Hold of Fear

Deliverance from all kinds of satanic bondages, including the spirit of the fear of death, is real. Apart from that, liberty is our covenant right in Christ Jesus. Hence, to be bound by anything all our lifetime is an error that needs to be corrected. We are no longer in Babylon, the epicentre of fear in the days of Israel. Jesus already bought our salvation, peace, and liberty with His own precious blood 2,000 years ago. It is not something you work for, but something you need to believe God for. Yes, you need Bible-rooted faith to walk in the reality of your redemption that came from the sacrifice that Christ Jesus made on the cross.

Galatians 3:13-14

Christ has redeemed us from the curse of the law, having become a curse for us (for it is written, "Cursed *is* everyone who hangs on a tree"), that the blessing of Abraham might come upon the Gentiles in Christ Jesus, that we might receive the promise of the Spirit through faith.

Isaiah 10:27 (KJV)

And it shall come to pass in that day, that his burden shall be taken away from off thy shoulder, and his yoke from off thy neck, and the yoke shall be destroyed because of the anointing.

Now concerning the woman I mentioned in this chapter, afflicted by the spirit of the fear of death. Well, when I prayed for her, she fell under the power of God, and her stomach part of the body twisted like a centipede. In fact, by that time, she was pregnant and expecting a baby. People of God, there is no devil, even the spirit of fear that can stand against the power of God in Christ Jesus. When she got up from the ground, that was the end of that satanic oppression. I believe God wants the best for our lives in Christ Jesus. Hence, we must always be encouraged to stand in our liberty, which Jesus Christ our Lord and Saviour secured for us on the cross.

Galatians 5:1

Stand fast therefore in the liberty by which Christ has made us free, and do not be entangled again with a yoke of bondage.

When you operate in fear, you become a covenant, or law breaker. Saints, we are called to walk according to the instructions of God's Word in Christ Jesus. Several times in the Scriptures, we are instructed to live and walk by faith and not fear. When you operate in fear, it means you are operating in doubt or unbelief. It further means you are doubting the ability of God, which is in Christ Jesus. That is the last thing the Holy One of Israel, our God in Heaven, would love to see in us. He is too faithful to fail — He is a covenant-keeping God. Besides, we did not receive the spirit of fear or of the devil for us to fear again.

2 Timothy 1:7

> For God has not given us a spirit of fear, but of power and of love and of a sound mind.

Many years ago, I was called upon to pray and anoint a house for a lady who used to have witchcraft attacks at night. Well, the protection is not in the oil—the anointing oil is just *symbolic* of our faith in God. Just like when God instructed the children of Israel to apply blood on the door lentils, the protection was not in the blood of the bulls they applied. Instead, the blood was just an expression of their faith and obedience to God. In fact, the lady was a Christian believer, but the devil tormented her life just like that. However, when I anointed her house with oil, that was the end of that affliction. I pray you won't be a victim of fear anymore, in Jesus' name.

Isaiah 54:17

No weapon formed against you shall prosper, And every tongue *which* rises against you in judgment You shall condemn. This *is* the heritage of the servants of the Lord, And their righteousness *is* from Me," Says the Lord.

May all the demons pursuing your life and destiny, even in your dreams, catch the fire of God and get destroyed in the name of Jesus!! God bless you!!

CHAPTER TWO

Spiritual Ignorance

Psalm 82:4-7

Deliver the poor and needy; Free *them* from the hand of the wicked. They do not know, nor do they understand; They walk about in darkness; All the foundations of the earth are unstable. I said, "You *are* gods, And all of you *are* children of the Most High. But you shall die like men, And fall like one of the princes."

Knowledge is Everything

What does the word *ignorance* mean? It means a lack of knowledge or information. Now, the ignorance we are talking about in this chapter concerns the knowledge of God's Word. Beloved, spiritual knowledge is everything in the Kingdom of God. The level at which you experience divine peace and liberty in Christ Jesus is a function of the knowledge of God's Word in your life. Remember this! No matter how much you are *born again* when you lack the knowledge of God's Word, that makes you become an ignorant person.

John 8:31-32

Then Jesus said to those Jews who believed Him, "If you abide in My word, you are My disciples indeed. And you shall know the truth, and the truth shall make you free."

There are certain prayers you don't need to pray once you have the knowledge of God's Word operable in your life at the revelation level. Just your presence is enough to destroy all powers of darkness, including fear. Jesus was the epitome of the knowledge of God's Word such that wherever He went, demons and devils came under the judgement of God. It was so powerful that devils, unclean spirits, and all powers of darkness begged Him not to destroy them before their time. Hence, if you don't know who you are in Christ Jesus, you will die like a mere man.

Saints, as long as we are in this world, we will always have an opportunity of walking in fear. However, walking in fear is not by superimposition, but by choice. Why? That is because God has given us His divine knowledge to walk in dominion over fear of any kind. There are people today who can't marry because of the fear of divorce. While others can't start a business for fear of failure. If you don't deal with fear in your life, you will become a liability. That is why, before you venture into any business, get rid of spiritual ignorance, because it is one enemy that can stop your destiny in Christ Jesus. Never tolerate it!

Hosea 4:6

My people are destroyed for lack of knowledge. Because you have rejected knowledge, I also will reject you from being priest for Me; Because you have forgotten the law of your God, I also will forget your children.

You can carry a gun that is supposed to give you victory or mastery over your enemies. However, if you don't know how to use it, and what it can do, you will die as a mere man or woman. Without a doubt, the primary reason people are weak in life today is because they lack God's divine knowledge in Christ Jesus. I have also met several people who are always tired in life. Why? Because they lack the knowledge of God's Word to give them strength. God's divine knowledge will always enable you to be a partaker of God's divine nature. Friends, spiritual knowledge is non-negotiable! Get it where you can find it under heaven!

Proverbs 23:23

Buy the truth, and do not sell *it, Also* wisdom and instruction and understanding.

2 Peter 1:3-4

As His divine power has given to us all things that *pertain* to life and godliness, through the knowledge of Him who called us by glory and virtue, by which have been given to us exceedingly great and precious promises, that through these you may be partakers of the divine nature, having escaped the corruption *that is* in the world through lust.

Proverbs 24:5

A wise man *is* strong, Yes, a man of knowledge increases strength.

You and I need adequate knowledge to overcome all the enemies of our destinies in Christ Jesus.

You Need to Wake Up!

I believe it is one thing to have knowledge and another to make it work for you. Many people have died young because of failure to put God's knowledge to work. It is possible to know what Jesus did for us on Calvary, yet we choose to do nothing about it. What is that? Spiritual laziness, blindness, and slumber! How do you explain a situation where someone knows the promises of God's Word of healing, success, and peace, yet they turn a deaf ear to the Word of God? Well, that is spiritual irresponsibility or slumber at work!

Always be careful with spiritual slumber, it has destroyed many lives of people. When God's children are asleep spiritually, that is the time the devil sneaks into their lives to sway them. I pray that won't be your portion in Jesus' name! Thus, any plant God has not planted in your life must get uprooted. You and I need a vigilant spirit to stop the devil's evil plans in our lives. Then, another way to stop the devil from invading our territories is by being spiritually informed or awake. Physical slumber is much better than the spiritual one. Of course, spiritual slumber will always stop your entire destiny from marching forward.

Matthew 13:24-25

Another parable He put forth to them, saying: "The kingdom of heaven is like a man who sowed good seed in his field; but while men slept, his enemy came and sowed tares among the wheat and went his way.

No matter your opinion, spiritual slumber will always assassinate your life and destiny in Christ Jesus. Why do you think King David fell into sexual sin? Was it because of a lack of spiritual knowledge? No! I believe it was spiritual slumber! Without a doubt, spiritual slumber has led many people into sin or sinful pleasures! I guess King David did not just fall into sexual sin overnight—it all started from somewhere! Perhaps his spiritual fellowship with God was down. Saints, it takes spiritual alertness to live above sin of any kind.

2 Samuel 11:1

It happened in the spring of the year, at the time when kings go out *to battle*, that David sent Joab and his servants with him, and all Israel; and they destroyed the people of Ammon and besieged Rabbah. But David remained at Jerusalem.

Friends, why do you think King David decided not to go to war or battle at the time when kings went out to battle? Often, people withdraw from spiritual engagement with God because of spiritual slumber or laziness. I believe that was the reason David did what he did. I pray spiritual slumber won't take over your life in Jesus' name! Instead, you will develop a vigilant spirit that will enable you to remain connected to God. Don't be slothful for any reason, please! Now, let us look at what happened to David next!

2 Samuel 11:1-5

It happened in the spring of the year, at the time when kings go out to battle, that David sent Joab and his servants with him, and all Israel; and they destroyed the people of Ammon and besieged Rabbah. But David remained at Jerusalem. Then it happened one evening that David arose from his bed and walked on the roof of the king's house. And from the roof he saw a woman bathing, and the woman was very beautiful to behold. So David sent and inquired about the woman. And someone said, "Is this not Bathsheba, the daughter of Eliam, the wife of Uriah the Hittite?" Then David sent messengers, and took her; and she came to him, and he lay with her, for she was cleansed from her impurity; and she returned to her house. And the woman conceived; so she sent and told David, and said, "I am with child."

Many pastors have lost churches to the devil because of spiritual slumber. Most of the time, pastors sleep spiritually and end up committing sexual sin. Then, because of that, it affects the spiritual condition of their flock or souls. For example, a pastor divorces his wife of twenty years in marriage for no Bible reasons, such as death or adultery. Some pastors will even claim God spoke to them. Well, did they have the knowledge of God concerning the hatred God has for divorce? Yes, they did! But what happened? Spiritual slumber! Or else we can say disobedience to God and His Word. Please wake up from your spiritual sleep, in Jesus' name!

Ephesians 5:11-14

And have no fellowship with the unfruitful works of darkness, but rather expose *them.* For it is shameful even to speak of those things which are done by them in secret. But all things that are exposed are made manifest by the light, for whatever makes manifest is light. Therefore He says: "Awake, you who sleep, Arise from the dead, And Christ will give you light."

You and I need to wake up from our spiritual slumber and get back to God henceforth.

Let Us Get Back to God

Are you telling me that Samson, the deliverer of Israel, didn't know that keeping company with a prostitute was not God's will? Yes, he did! But what happened? I believe it was equally the case of spiritual slumber. Sadly, it cost him his entire life! Delilah, the prostitute, knew what she was after. Saints, life is the most precious thing God has given us. Thus, let us guard it with all diligence. It was the time when Samson woke up from his sleep that he realised God had left him. Many people, even Christians, don't know that God has left them. Why? Because of spiritual slumber! I pray God will open your spiritual eyes in Jesus' name.

Judges 16:1-3, 20-21

Now Samson went to Gaza and saw a harlot there, and went in to her. *When* the Gazites *were told,* "Samson has come here!" they surrounded *the place* and lay in wait for him all night at the gate of the city. They were quiet all night, saying, "In the morning, when it is daylight, we will kill him." And Samson lay *low* till midnight; then he arose at midnight, took hold of the doors of the gate of the city and the two gateposts, pulled them up, bar and all, put *them* on his shoulders, and carried them to the top of the hill that faces Hebron.

There was a time in the life of Samson when he could lay hold of the doors of the gate of a city. He pulled them up, put them on his shoulders, and carried them to the top of the hills. Of course, when you are spiritually awake, there is always divine energy in your life to do impossible things. However, when you slumber spiritually or fall into sin, you lose the power of God. Each time you tolerate sin in your life, it gains dominance over you. Hence, when Samson compromised his spiritual life, he lost sensitivity to God and His power. I pray you won't fall into the trap of the devil. Let's look at what happened to Samson next.

Judges 16:18-21

> When Delilah saw that he had told her all his heart, she sent and called for the lords of the Philistines, saying, "Come up once more, for he has told me all his heart." So

the lords of the Philistines came up to her and brought the money in their hand. Then she lulled him to sleep on her knees, and called for a man and had him shave off the seven locks of his head. Then she began to torment him, and his strength left him. And she said, "The Philistines *are* upon you, Samson!" So he awoke from his sleep, and said, "I will go out as before, at other times, and shake myself free!" But he did not know that the Lord had departed from him. Then the Philistines took him and put out his eyes, and brought him down to Gaza. They bound him with bronze fetters, and he became a grinder in the prison.

People of God, each time you fall into sin for any apparent reason, repentance is the only way back to God. No matter where you live, whether in Africa, Australia, Europe, Asia, South America, or the USA, don't waste time getting back to

God when you miss it in life. Also, when you know things are not working for you, get back to God for correction and guidance. You don't need to justify yourself. Just get back to God in humility and ask for His forgiveness, mercy, and grace. Self-justification is dangerous! When Samson repented, God forgave him and restored His power back to him.

Judges 16:28-30

Then Samson called to the Lord, saying, "O Lord God, remember me, I pray! Strengthen me, I pray, just this once, O God, that I may with one *blow* take vengeance on the Philistines for my two eyes!" And Samson took hold of the two middle pillars which supported the temple, and he braced himself against them, one on his right and the other on his left. Then Samson said, "Let me die with the Philistines!" And he pushed with *all his* might, and the temple fell on the lords and all the people who *were* in it. So the dead that he killed at his death were more than he had killed in his life.

No matter the wrong you have done in life, getting back to God in humility and repentance is the only way to restoration. Yes, it is the only way to fulfil your destiny in a grand style in Christ Jesus. God bless you!!

CHAPTER THREE

Disobedience

Ephesians 2:1-3

And you *He made alive,* who were dead in trespasses and sins, in which you once walked according to the course of this world, according to the prince of the power of the air, the spirit who now works in the sons of disobedience, among whom also we all once conducted ourselves in the lusts of our flesh, fulfilling the desires of the flesh and of the mind, and were by nature children of wrath, just as the others.

The Spirit of Disobedience

I believe disobedience is a spirit, and it cannot get superimposed on you. Instead, it is a choice you make! Thus, you can't say the devil made you walk in disobedience or sin. No! Now, what is disobedience? Well, according to the *Oxford dictionary,* disobedience is failure or refusal to obey rules or someone in authority. Disobedience has the potential to stop your life and destiny from marching forward in Christ Jesus. The disobedience we are talking about here is the one where you disobey God and His Word. Saints, the only way to preserve your destiny from corruption is by walking in obedience to God and His Word.

Deuteronomy 28:1-2

"Now it shall come to pass, if you diligently obey the voice of the Lord your God, to observe carefully all His commandments which I command you today, that the Lord your God will set you high above all nations of the earth. And all these blessings shall come upon you and overtake you, because you obey the voice of the Lord your God.

If you want to last long in life, you must always desire to walk in obedience to God and His Word. It doesn't matter what you have today in life, disobedience can bring you down. The disobedient people do not have a place in the school of greatness or victory. Saints, if you want to go very far in life, obeying God and His Word is the way to go. I pray you won't reach a point in your life where you become too big to walk in obedience to God and His Word. For example, in the Bible, there were so many kings that God elevated, but because of disobedience, they became nothing. Let us have a look at some of those kings.

(1) King Saul

King Saul was, according to the Hebrew Bible, the first monarch of the United Kingdom of Israel. He started very well and ruled Israel for over forty years. Sadly, he was rejected as a king by God because of his disobedience. Thus, disobedience is one of the enemies of your destiny, even today. King Saul's destiny was cut short, and God tore away the kingdom from Him and gave it to David. Obeying God will always take you to the top of life while disobeying Him and His Word will bring your entire life and destiny down in no time. Just be careful!

1 Samuel 15: 10-11, 22, 27-28

Now the word of the Lord came to Samuel, saying, "I greatly regret that I have set up Saul *as* king, for he has turned back from following Me, and has not performed My commandments." And it grieved Samuel, and he cried out to the Lord all night. So Samuel said: "Has the Lord *as great* delight in burnt offerings and sacrifices, As in obeying the voice of the Lord? Behold, to obey is better than sacrifice, *And* to heed than the fat of rams. And as Samuel turned around to go away, *Saul* seized the edge of his robe, and it tore. So Samuel said to him, "The Lord has torn the kingdom of Israel from you today, and has given it to a neighbor of yours, *who is* better than you.

People of God, in the above Scripture, King Saul lost his destiny in a split moment because of disobeying God's commandment. Whether in Africa, Australia, Asia, Europe, or the USA, disobedience to God and His commandments will reduce your life to nothing. It is a destiny killer and has no place in heaven or the Kingdom of God. Stay away from it!!

(2). King Solomon

1 Kings 3:3-5

> And Solomon loved the Lord, walking in the statutes of his father David, except that he sacrificed and burned incense at the high places. Now the king went to Gibeon to sacrifice there, for that *was* the great high place: Solomon offered a thousand burnt offerings on that altar. At Gibeon the Lord appeared to Solomon in a dream by night; and God said, "Ask! What shall I give you?"

Beloved, without a doubt, King Solomon began well with God, but his end was terrible! God favoured Solomon by making him a king based on the covenant that God made with his father, David. Friends, it is one thing to start well and another to finish well and strong. Hence, Jesus said that those who shall endure up to the end shall be saved (Matthew 24:13). What does that mean? It means that as much as you start your life well with God, make sure you endure up to the end. People have sold their souls to Satan because of the pleasures of this world. One reason Solomon turned his back on God was because of women.

1 Kings 11: 6, 9-11

Solomon did evil in the sight of the Lord, and did not fully follow the Lord, as *did* his father David. So the Lord became angry with Solomon, because his heart had turned from the Lord God of Israel, who had appeared to him twice, and had commanded him concerning this thing, that he should not go after other gods; but he did not keep what the Lord had commanded. Therefore the Lord said to Solomon, "Because you have done this, and have not kept My covenant and My statutes, which I have commanded you, I will surely tear the kingdom away from you and give it to your servant.

My prayer is that walking in obedience to God and His Word will become your number one priority in life. You will delight in God's divine commandments, guidance, instructions, correction, and reproof in Christ Jesus. God bless you!!

(3). King Uzziah

Another king who began well but drifted away from God and walked in sin or disobedience was Uzziah. King Uzziah (also known as Azariah) was one of the greatest kings of Judah. In many ways, he honoured God, and he had a lot of success and power. Yet even good kings have their problems, and Uzziah doesn't end well. He died a leper and a disgrace because he could not handle his success and power. God's people disobeying God is the most dreadful thing in life. Besides, disobedience can send you to Hell if you don't repent. Without a doubt, King Uzziah began very well, and God prospered him, but his end was not well.

2 Chronicles 26: 3-5

Uzziah *was* sixteen years old when he became king, and he reigned fifty-two years in Jerusalem. His mother's name was Jecholiah of Jerusalem. And he did *what was* right in the sight of the Lord, according to all that his father Amaziah had done. He sought God in the days of Zechariah, who had understanding in the visions of God; and as long as he sought the Lord, God made him prosper.

People of God, it is not how you start that matters, but how you finish. I know many people who began well—walking in God's fear — giants of faith in Christ Jesus but gave up on God. Sadly, King Uzziah died a leper—God was angry with him. May you walk in the fear of God all the days of your life henceforth!

2 Chronicles 26:16-18

But when he was strong his heart was lifted up, to *his* destruction, for he transgressed against the Lord his God by entering the temple of the Lord to burn incense on the altar of incense. So Azariah the priest went in after him, and with him were eighty priests of the Lord–valiant men. And they withstood King Uzziah, and said to him, "*It is* not for you, Uzziah, to burn incense to the Lord, but for the priests, the sons of Aaron, who are consecrated to burn incense. Get out of the sanctuary, for you have trespassed! You *shall have* no honor from the Lord God."

When God dishonours you because of your disobedience, that is the end of your life and destiny!

2 Chronicles 26:19-21

Then Uzziah became furious; and he *had* a censer in his hand to burn incense. And while he was angry with the priests, leprosy broke out on his forehead, before the priests in the house of the Lord, beside the incense altar. And Azariah the chief priest and all the priests looked at him, and there, on his forehead, he *was* leprous; so they thrust him out of that place. Indeed he also hurried to get out, because the Lord had struck him. King Uzziah was a leper until the day of his death. He dwelt in an isolated house, because he was a leper; for he was cut off from the house of the Lord. Then Jotham his son *was* over the king's house, judging the people of the land.

May you walk to please God all the days of your life in Christ Jesus!!

Stay Away from Disobedience!

Romans 1:1-6

Paul, a bondservant of Jesus Christ, called *to be* an apostle, separated to the gospel of God which He promised before through His prophets in the Holy Scriptures, concerning His Son Jesus Christ our Lord, who was born of the seed of David according to the flesh, *and* declared *to be* the Son of God with power according to the Spirit of holiness, by the resurrection from the dead. Through Him we have received grace and apostleship for obedience to the faith among all nations for His name, among whom you also are the called of Jesus Christ.

The call to walk in obedience and holiness to God does not mean you become sinless. Only Jesus Christ, our Lord and Saviour, is sinless! Hence, He died and shed His blood on the cross to remove sin away from us! Above all; we have also received grace and apostleship to walk in obedience to God and His Word. Hence, failure to walk in obedience to God and His counsel is a choice. Nothing else! Saints, walking in obedience to God and His Word is the only way to preserve your life and destiny. Yes, obedience to God will set you above all devils and demons. Even Jesus, it was His obedience to God that exalted Him above all things.

Philippians 2: 5-11

Let this mind be in you which was also in Christ Jesus, who, being in the form of God, did not consider it robbery to be equal with God, but made Himself of no reputation, taking the form of a bondservant, *and* coming in the likeness of men. And being found in appearance as a man, He humbled Himself and became obedient to *the point of* death, even the death of the cross. Therefore God also has highly exalted Him and given Him the name which is above every name, that at the name of Jesus every knee should bow, of those in heaven, and of those on earth, and of those under the earth, and *that* every tongue should confess that Jesus Christ *is* Lord, to the glory of God the Father.

Our obedience to God will always bring glory to Him. If you want to attract God's divine presence, then walk and live to obey

God. Obey God in your giving, in your lifestyle, in your entire soul, mind, body, and spirit. If you refuse to stay away from disobedience, the Holy Spirit won't be in your environment. Obedience is the only key that can unlock any hopeless door to your destiny. Hence, Jesus was obedient to God up to the point of His death. That is not to be taken lightly—it is such a serious thing. Adam and Eve got kicked out of the Garden of Eden after they disobeyed God. Disobedience will always dethrone you from God's glory.

Genes 3:22-24

Then the Lord God said, "Behold, the man has become like one of Us, to know good and evil. And now, lest he put out his hand and take also of the tree of life, and eat, and live forever"– therefore the Lord God sent him out of the garden of Eden to till the ground from which he was taken. So He drove out the man; and He placed cherubim at the east of the garden of Eden, and a flaming sword which turned every way, to guard the way to the tree of life.

I pray that your desire to obey God and His Word will multiply in your life in Jesus' name.

CHAPTER FOUR

Unbelief

James 1:5-8

If any of you lacks wisdom, let him ask of God, who gives to all liberally and without reproach, and it will be given to him. But let him ask in faith, with no doubting, for he who doubts is like a wave of the sea driven and tossed by the wind. For let not that man suppose that he will receive anything from the Lord; *he is* a double-minded man, unstable in all his ways.

Unbelief is a Destiny Killer

If you want your destiny to stop marching forward, then allow unbelief to have its way into your life. Unbelief is against Jesus, against the Word of God, and the Holy Spirit. The reason unbelief is the enemy of your destiny is because it opposes God's will. It will always argue and treat God's Word with levity. When your mind is not submissive to the Word of God, just know that it is unbelief at work. Sometimes, you may convince yourself that you have faith, but unbelief is in your mind working. Look, when Jesus went to His hometown, could not do any mighty miracle because of people's unbelief. Unbelief is a destiny killer!

Mark 6:16

> Then He went out from there and came to His own country, and His disciples followed Him. And when the Sabbath had come, He began to teach in the synagogue. And many hearing *Him* were astonished, saying, "Where *did* this Man *get* these

things? And what wisdom *is* this which is given to Him, that such mighty works are performed by His hands! Is this not the carpenter, the Son of Mary, and brother of James, Joses, Judas, and Simon? And are not His sisters here with us?" So they were offended at Him. But Jesus said to them, "A prophet is not without honor except in his own country, among his own relatives, and in his own house." Now He could do no mighty work there, except that He laid His hands on a few sick people and healed *them*. And He marveled because of their unbelief. Then He went about the villages in a circuit, teaching.

Jesus Christ, who is also the Word of God, went to His hometown, but could not do any mighty miracle because of the people's unbelief. Each time you are praying and expecting a miracle from God, always check the state of your mind. It is possible to have faith in your heart, but still have unbelief in your mind. Many years ago, I prayed for an entrepreneur who was experiencing satanic oppression. Now, while praying for him, it was like hitting against the wall. By then, I had been praying for many people over the years and saw significant results. However, with him, nothing was happening at all—I struggled with it!

Then, I eventually discovered that the man never believed God could use me to help him get delivered. Saints, no matter your prayers, if people can't believe in God, don't waste your time praying for anything. Why? That is because nothing will happen—unbelief is a destiny killer and blocker. I don't think you and I can outwit the anointing that was upon Jesus. He could not do any mighty miracle in His hometown because of unbelief. Hence, the Bible says he that comes to God must believe and without faith; it is impossible to please God. Walking in unbelief is wickedness—it will make your heart evil. Don't entertain it!

Hebrews 11:5-6

By faith Enoch was taken away so that he did not see death, "and was not found, because God had taken him"; for before he was taken he had this testimony, that he pleased God. But without faith *it is* impossible to please *Him,* for he who comes to God must believe that He is, and *that* He is a rewarder of those who diligently seek Him.

The message of faith is not just an encouragement. No! Instead, it is such a serious thing to God and His divine operations in Christ Jesus. There is no way God can crown you with His glory if you will entertain unbelief in your life. Many people's destinies are stagnant today because of the spirit of unbelief at work in their lives. The spirit of unbelief is like poison. It will kill your spiritual sensitivity and connection to God. Yes, poison will kill you once allowed in your bloodstream. Friends, the beauty of your destiny is a function of your faith in God. Hence, if you need help with your faith, don't waste time. Instead, go for it!

Mark 9:20-24

Then they brought him to Him. And when he saw Him, immediately the spirit convulsed him, and he fell on the ground and wallowed, foaming at the mouth. So He asked his father, "How long has this been happening to him?" And he said, "From childhood. And often he has thrown him both into the fire and into the water to destroy him. But if You can do anything, have compassion on us and help us." Jesus said to him, "If you can believe, all things *are* possible to him who believes." Immediately the father of the child cried out and said with tears, "Lord, I believe; help my unbelief!"

People of God, never allow unbelief at any point in your life. It is a destiny killer and destroyer!

People Died in the Wilderness

There is nothing that God hates, like unbelief. I have seen many lives of people get destroyed over the years because of unbelief. It doesn't matter which country you live in, walking in unbelief is ungodliness, as it works against the will of God. You may have terrible moments in your life, but don't tolerate the spirit of unbelief. Unbelief has everything to do with your mind stepping back into the realm of doubt, where God's power and sovereignty get undermined. There was a lady who came into our church expecting the blessing of the womb. Sadly, within a short time, she left our church. Why? I believe it was the spirit of unbelief that was at work in her life. Yes, unbelief is always impatient and will make your heart evil!

Hebrews 3:7-12

Therefore, as the Holy Spirit says: "Today, if you will hear His voice, Do not harden your hearts as in the rebellion, In the day of trial in the wilderness, Where your fathers tested Me, tried Me, And saw My works forty years. Therefore I was angry with that generation, And said, 'They always go astray in *their* heart, And they have not known My ways.' So I swore in My wrath, 'They shall not enter My rest.' " Beware, brethren, lest there be in any of you an evil heart of unbelief in departing from the living God.

Beloved, unbelief will stop your life the quickest and bring shame into your environment. In fact, when you look at the Scripture above, God had sworn upon Himself to never give rest to Israel because of unbelief. Wherever you sense a restlessness in your life, it could be unbelief at work in your life. Apart from that, unbelief is a spirit, and it is contagious—stay away from it! Choose your friendships wisely! The last thing God will ever want to hear is for His creation to reduce Him, even in their thinking. Most of the people in transit to the Promised Land never made it there. Why? Because they entertained unbelief in their lives.

Hebrews 3:16-19

For who, having heard, rebelled? Indeed, *was it* not all who came out of Egypt, *led* by Moses? Now with whom was He angry forty years? *Was it* not with those

> who sinned, whose corpses fell in the wilderness? And to whom did He swear that they would not enter His rest, but to those who did not obey? So we see that they could not enter in because of unbelief.

Unbelief will always harden your heart such that you can't even listen to God's divine counsel. When you see people can't receive divine counsel, instead, all they want is their own way. Just know it is the spirit of unbelief at work. Also, the spirit of unbelief has its source in disobedience to God's knowledge. If you can't receive God's Word with meekness, you will soon allow the entrance of unbelief into your life. If you can't subject your mind to the Word of God, you will soon open a door to the spirit of unbelief. Hence, today we have so many people in church who are under satanic oppression because of unbelief. Coming to church is not the answer to the spirit of unbelief, but the revelations of God's Word coming into your life.

Ephesians 1:15-18

Therefore I also, after I heard of your faith in the Lord Jesus and your love for all the saints, do not cease to give thanks for you, making mention of you in my prayers: that the God of our Lord Jesus Christ, the Father of glory, may give to you the spirit of wisdom and revelation in the knowledge of Him, the eyes of your understanding being enlightened; that you may know what is the hope of His calling, what are the riches of the glory of His inheritance in the saints.

My prayer is that the Holy Spirit will empower you to overcome unbelief in your life henceforth.

Unbelief Corrupts Destiny

Unbelief has the potential to corrupt your destiny, which is in Christ Jesus. If you want your destiny to speak the loudest in your life, then never entertain unbelief. To have your destiny corrupted should be the last thing to think of or imagine in your life. Many people's destinies, even Christians, got corrupted because of unbelief at work in their lives. The destiny of Thomas, Jesus' disciple, almost got corrupted because of unbelief in his life. If you don't deal with unbelief, it will eventually become the entry point of all demonic activities in your life. People of God, there is a blessing that comes with believing God and His Word.

John 20:24-29

> Now Thomas, called the Twin, one of the twelve, was not with them when Jesus

came. The other disciples therefore said to him, "We have seen the Lord." So he said to them, "Unless I see in His hands the print of the nails, and put my finger into the print of the nails, and put my hand into His side, I will not believe." And after eight days His disciples were again inside, and Thomas with them. Jesus came, the doors being shut, and stood in the midst, and said, "Peace to you!" Then He said to Thomas, "Reach your finger here, and look at My hands; and reach your hand *here,* and put *it* into My side. Do not be unbelieving, but believing." And Thomas answered and said to Him, "My Lord and my God!" Jesus said to him, "Thomas, because you have seen Me, you have believed. Blessed *are* those who have not seen and *yet* have believed."

Just because you are a preacher or pastor does not mean that you won't have any *unbelief* problems. Thomas, called *"Didymus"*, Jesus' disciple, was among the twelve doing ministry with Jesus. He saw all the miracles Jesus did, but unbelief was at work in his life. It is not about the title that you have that matters, but an encounter with God and His Word. Abraham, our patriarchy, and the father of faith, believed in God because of the encounters he had with God and His holy presence. Hence, the Bible says he did not waver through unbelief. Instead, he was strong in faith up to the point of God's divine visitation in his life.

> **Romans 4:17-21**
>
> (as it is written, "I have made you a father of many nations") in the presence of Him whom he believed–God, who gives life to the dead and calls those things which do not exist as though they did; who, contrary

to hope, in hope believed, so that he became the father of many nations, according to what was spoken, "So shall your descendants be." And not being weak in faith, he did not consider his own body, already dead (since he was about a hundred years old), and the deadness of Sarah's womb. He did not waver at the promise of God through unbelief, but was strengthened in faith, giving glory to God, and being fully convinced that what He had promised He was also able to perform.

If you allow unbelief to dominate your life, then you have no future at all. Unbelief will also open a door to the spirit of fear, and fear is one of the enemies of destiny. One reason Moses couldn't enter the Promised Land was because of unbelief. Was not Moses a man of faith? Yes, he was—to go into Egypt and deliver God's people you need faith. To stand before the Red Sea waiting for it to open while your enemies are coming behind you will always require faith. Of course, you can have faith in your life, but at some point, allow unbelief. When Moses hit the rock instead of speaking to it, it was regarded by God as unbelief at work.

Numbers 20:10-12

And Moses and Aaron gathered the assembly together before the rock; and he said to them, "Hear now, you rebels! Must we bring water for you out of this rock?" Then Moses lifted his hand and struck the rock twice with his rod; and water came out abundantly, and the congregation and their animals drank. Then the Lord spoke to Moses and Aaron, "Because you did not believe Me, to hallow Me in the eyes of the children of Israel, therefore you shall not bring this assembly into the land which I have given them."

Entertaining unbelief in your life will always corrupt your life and destiny. Hence, you must come against it in Jesus' name. God bless you!!

CHAPTER FIVE

Laziness

Proverbs 24:30-34

I went by the field of the lazy *man*, And by the vineyard of the man devoid of understanding; And there it was, all overgrown with thorns; Its surface was covered with nettles; Its stone wall was broken down. When I saw *it*, I considered *it* well; I looked on *it and* received instruction: A little sleep, a little slumber, A little folding of the hands to rest; So shall your poverty come *like* a prowler, And your need like an armed man.

Hard Work Pays Off

I don't know about you, but one thing I know is that laziness is one of the major enemies of destiny in Christ Jesus. Now, when I talk of laziness, I mean in every area of your life. Someone can be lazy at finding work to support himself and his family. While others can be lazy in pursuing God. Whatever it is, laziness will always slow down your life and destiny. Whether in Africa, Europe, Asia, Australia, South America, or the USA, lazy people have no place in the school of success and prosperity. Wherever you find lazy people, you will also find poverty at work. God's will for us is to be hardworking and responsible people.

Being lazy does not mean being ignorant. I know many knowledgeable and qualified people who are lazy and have become liabilities to society. Of course, you can know what to do in life but still be lazy. Many people, even Christians, think demonic activities are the reason for their laziness. Well, there are cases where laziness can be attributed to demonic activities in our lives. However, most of the time, laziness is a behaviour or an attitude that we often cultivate in our own lives. Now, just like people can cultivate laziness, they can equally cultivate hard work. For example, I learnt to be hardworking from my father when I was just a young man. Yes, I cultivated it in the early stage of my life. Saints, to every labour, there is profit, while to every laziness, there is poverty.

Proverbs 14:23

> In all labor there is profit, But idle chatter *leads* only to poverty.

Hard work will always pay you off! Now, when I talk of hard work, I don't mean coming to a place in your life where you forget about God and His Word. Hardworking without engaging God in your life won't take you anywhere. Many Christians, by trying to work hard, neglect God and His Word. Failure to engage Jesus in anything you are doing is a risk. We live in a dispensation of time where human effort has become more important than God's presence. I believe engaging God at every stage of your life is the safest thing to do as a child of God. Without Jesus in our lives, we can do nothing, no matter our opinions.

John 15:5

> "I am the vine, you *are* the branches. He who abides in Me, and I in him, bears much fruit; for without Me you can do nothing.

Prayer and giving are powerful and outstanding virtues in Christ Jesus! However, if you and I are idle in life, doing nothing, we will remain poor. Laziness will never change our financial position, no matter how much we pray. You and I can't rely on prayer alone to get money. Instead, we need to do something practically with our hands, preceded by faith, prayer, creativity, knowledge, understanding and wisdom. Sadly, many people, even Christians, blame God for poverty in their lives. Well, God is not the cause of our poverty! His desire is for us to walk in abundance, which is in Christ Jesus, our Lord and Saviour.

The Bible talks of the four lepers at the entrance of the gates of Samaria. Now, being lepers, they fed on leftovers from within the city. Sadly, there was a time when Samaria experienced a famine because of the drought in the land. The famine was terrible such that people ate people! It was even worse for the lepers because leftovers were not coming to the gates of Samaria. However, being lepers was not the reason for them to be lazy and die of starvation. Instead, they found a way out of that situation through hard work and divine intervention. I pray your hard work will attract God's presence in your life.

2 Kings 7:3-5

Now there were four leprous men at the entrance of the gate; and they said to one another, "Why are we sitting here until we die? ⁴ If we say, 'We will enter the city,' the famine *is* in the city, and we shall die there. And if we sit here, we die also. Now therefore, come, let us surrender to the army of the Syrians. If they keep us alive, we shall live; and if they kill us, we shall only die." ⁵ And they rose at twilight to go to the camp of the Syrians; and when they had come to the outskirts of the Syrian camp, to their surprise no one *was* there.

Friends, just like the lepers in the above Scripture, hard work will always give you a place of honour in this world. What happened to the lepers was a miracle provoked by hardworking, God's divine favour and mercy. Let us look at what happened next.

2 Kings 7: 7-8

Therefore they arose and fled at twilight, and left the camp intact–their tents, their horses, and their donkeys–and they fled for their lives. And when these lepers came to the outskirts of the camp, they went into one tent and ate and drank, and carried from it silver and gold and clothing, and went and hid *them;* then they came back and entered another tent, and carried *some* from there *also,* and went and hid *it.*

May you work hard in Jesus' name!

Laziness is Not God's Will

There is nothing good about laziness at all. God hates it! He never created you and me to occupy the seat or realm of laziness. No! When He created man (Adam), He set him over the entire affairs of the Garden of Eden. The Bible says in Genesis 2:15: ***Then the Lord God took the man and put him in the Garden of Eden to tend and keep it.*** Hardworking is in God's divine calendar for all humanity, even all His children in the faith. Hence, if you want to ascend to the top of your life and destiny in Christ Jesus, avoid being lazy!

I remember when I was doing my secondary education at a boarding school. There was a student who used to sleep throughout the entire school term. What that means is that he spent most of his time in bed sleeping, doing nothing. He did not attend most of the classes for lessons. At least everyone knew him for that.

Hence, he got the lowest and most embarrassing results in the entire school when the results came out. Beloved, you can't cheat life—it will deliver according to what you give it. That is why we must stop blaming God, even the devil, for our laziness and failure! Let us wake up and work very hard!

Proverbs 6:9-11

How long will you slumber, O sluggard? When will you rise from your sleep? A little sleep, a little slumber, A little folding of the hands to sleep- So shall your poverty come.

When I talk of laziness, I don't mean the one-day thing, but the one embedded in your DNA. Of course, sometimes you can feel lazy to do a few things in life— it is acceptable! However, when laziness becomes your lifestyle, that one is dangerous. Sometimes, laziness can attach itself to you, propelled by the devil and his cohorts. I pray God will open your spiritual eyes to see how laziness can stop your destiny from marching forward. Even Jesus was a hard worker—He used to work tirelessly! Many times, he would ask his disciples to meet him on the other side of the sea. He was committed to doing the work of His Father in Heaven.

John 9: 1-7

Now as *Jesus* passed by, He saw a man who was blind from birth. And His disciples asked Him, saying, "Rabbi, who sinned, this man or his parents, that he was born blind?" Jesus answered, "Neither this man nor his parents sinned, but that the works of God should be revealed in him. I must work the works of Him who sent Me while it is day; *the* night is coming when no one can work. As long as I am in the world, I am the light of the world." When He had said these things, He spat on the ground and made clay with the saliva; and He anointed the eyes of the blind man with the clay. And He said to him, "Go, wash in the pool of Siloam" (which is translated, Sent). So he went and washed, and came back seeing.

Sadly, the spirit of laziness has robbed the destinies of many people, even Christians. To remain a lazy person after you have known the truth is a choice. You can't harvest what you have not rendered the service for. Doing that is what we can call *robbery* or *stealing*, and the only place for thieves is jail or prison. However, the only time you can reap where you did not plant, or sow is when God gives you a miracle by supernatural intervention. Even when that happens, God will have suspended the laws of harvest which demand your hard work just to favour you. However, we can't force God to do that for us every time. If God doesn't move that way, then we need to do something with our hands by His grace.

Ephesians 4:28

Let him who stole steal no longer, but rather let him labor, working with *his* hands what is good, that he may have something to give him who has need.

1 Thessalonians 2:9

For you remember, brethren, our labor and toil; for laboring night and day, that we might not be a burden to any of you, we preached to you the gospel of God.

I pray that laziness won't be in your attitude or lifestyle in your life, in Jesus' name!

Overcoming Laziness

Without a doubt, you and I can overcome laziness in our lives. All we need is spiritual understanding! Otherwise, laziness can deprive us of a glorious life and future, if tolerated. Sometimes, you can be lazy without even knowing it. Then, the entrance of laziness in your life will always lead to poverty. There are many people today who just need to work extra hard to overcome poverty. Hard work will always dignify you and dethrone poverty in your life. Everything in the Kingdom of God thrives on the wheels of responsibility and hard work. Besides, God can only bless the works of your hands. It is a divine principle or law!

Deuteronomy 28:12-13

The Lord will open to you His good treasure, the heavens, to give the rain to your land in its season, and to bless all the work of your hand. You shall lend to many nations, but you shall not borrow. And the Lord will make you the head and not the tail; you shall be above only, and not be beneath, if you heed the commandments of the Lord your God, which I command you today, and are careful to observe *them*.

No one can outgrow the divine laws or principles of hard work. Asking for handouts in your life from one meeting to another is not your portion henceforth. The diligent will always reign in life while the lazy will starve and end up as beggars. God did not create you and me to be beggars—instead, to be lenders! Each time God wants to change your life or level, all He does is bless the works of your hands. Hence, if you are doing nothing, you will remain a gallant failure in life and destiny. Nothing more and nothing less!!

Deuteronomy 2:7

"For the Lord your God has blessed you in all the work of your hand. He knows your [trudging through this great wilderness. These forty years the Lord your God *has been* with you; you have lacked nothing." '

Beloved, you and I can overcome laziness! One way to triumph over laziness is for you to discover your worth and purpose in life. Now, if you know your worth and purpose, and you are still lazy, you need deliverance or spiritual help. Why? That is because if people, even Christians, don't know their worth or purpose, they lose the passion to do anything in life. They see themselves as failures—they become idle minds. Hence, when you see the youth doing nothing in society, just know that they need help. Nothing else!

Then, the other way to overcome laziness in your life as a child of God is for you to stay away from bad company. The company you keep determines what accompanies you. The people you mingle with will always determine where you end up in life. People of God, association determines acceleration! Can two people walk together unless they agree? (Amos 3:3). Certainly, there is a huge correlation between your future and the people you hang around with. If you hang around with thieves, you will soon become one, then if you hang around with witches, you will soon start practising witchcraft. May God have mercy on us!

1 Corinthians 15:33-34 (AMP)

Do not be deceived: "Bad company corrupts good morals." Be sober-minded [be sensible, wake up from your spiritual stupor] as you ought, and stop sinning; for some [of you] have no knowledge of God [you are disgracefully ignorant of Him, and ignore His truths]. I say this to your shame.

I have seen people who were hardworking change direction and become lazy people. Stay away from the evil company and your destiny will keep on shining. If you join the company of prostitutes, you will soon become a prostitute. If you join a company of spectators doing nothing in life, you will end up as a beggar at the time of harvest. Stop wasting your days or time by being a busybody—all you do is talk — doing nothing. Many people don't know that laziness is a mentality and needs a mind overhaul. No matter what you do with lazy people, they will remain lazy if they don't get their minds renewed in Christ Jesus. A lazy person will still be lazy whether they are in Africa, Australia, Europe, Asia, South America, or the USA.

Proverbs 20:4 (AMP)

The lazy man does not plow when the winter [planting] season arrives; So he begs at the [next] harvest and has nothing [to reap].

My prayer is that laziness won't be your portion henceforth in Jesus' name.

CHAPTER SIX

Pride

Revelation 12:7-9

And war broke out in heaven: Michael and his angels fought with the dragon; and the dragon and his angels fought, but they did not prevail, nor was a place found for them in heaven any longer. So the great dragon was cast out, that serpent of old, called the Devil and Satan, who deceives the whole world; he was cast to the earth, and his angels were cast out with him.

Pride Will Bring You Down

Beloved, the thing that brought the devil down was pride. Hence, there was no place found for him in Heaven. No matter who you are today, pride will always bring you down. If only you and I could understand who the Devil was before his fall from Heaven, then we would know exactly how destructive pride can be. The devil's original name was *Lucifer*. What does Lucifer mean? Well, the original Hebrew word means "shining one, light-bearer." It refers to his former splendour as the greatest of the angels. Sadly, he wanted to lift himself above God and wanted to become like God. Then, he got cast down here on Earth as profane.

Isaiah 14:12-15

"How you are fallen from heaven, O Lucifer, son of the morning! *How* you are cut down to the ground, You who weakened the nations! For you have said in your heart: 'I will ascend into heaven, I will exalt my throne above the stars of God; I will also sit on the mount of the congregation On the farthest sides of the north; I will ascend above the heights of the clouds, I will be like the Most High.' Yet you shall be brought down to Sheol, To the lowest depths of the Pit.

Without a doubt, God hates pride and the proud have no place in His Kingdom. That is why pride is one of the greatest enemies of destiny. Proud people never go far in life, neither do they last long. You will go out on the streets, and you won't find them at all. Hence, to remain relevant in the journey of life as a child of God, you must always make sure that you put pride away from your life. Great destinies have fallen because of pride. When you see a proud person, just know his or her days are numbered. The proud has the same destination as the lazy. I pray you won't tolerate it in your life in Jesus' name!

Proverbs 6:16 -19

These six *things* the Lord hates, Yes, seven *are* an abomination to Him: A proud look, A lying tongue, Hands that shed innocent blood, A heart that devises wicked plans, Feet that are swift in running to evil, A false witness *who* speaks lies, And one who sows discord among brethren.

One reason God hates pride is that it is an abomination to Him. We live in a dispensation of time in human history where pride is on the rise. When you see people having an attitude towards God's Word by putting trust in their riches, that is pride. When you say that you don't need God, you are okay. That is pride! Regrettably, many people nowadays pretend to be okay in life without Jesus. Why? Well, most of them put their trust in earthly riches or material possessions. Some of them don't even go to church — they feel too big to repent! Hence, many marriages have ended in divorce because of pride at work.

Saints, we live in perilous times where many people have embraced pride as a way of life. If you are a child of God, I encourage you to stay away from pride, as it will destroy your entire life and destiny. Many people, even Christians, have died early because of pride. Many years ago, we were evangelising as a church. Then, I came across one man who had a serious disease in his body and had only a few months to live. Now, as I spoke to him, I felt a strong healing anointing come upon me. Then I asked him if I could pray for him to receive healing from God. Unfortunately, he did not want to be prayed for—

he rejected my invitation. Well, I believe that was the spirit of pride at work—it takes humility to receive from God.

Proverbs 29:23

A man's pride will bring him low, But the humble in spirit will retain honor.

James 4:5-8

Or do you think that the Scripture says in vain, "The Spirit who dwells in us yearns jealously"? But He gives more grace. Therefore He says: "God resists the proud, But gives grace to the humble."

Some people think they are smarter than God's Word. What do they do next? Well, they want to add and subtract from God's Word. When you are deeply loyal to God and His Word, your life will scale heights of greatness in Christ Jesus. The Word of

God is not there for us to analyse or talk about, but to obey. The proud will always become objects of God's wrath if they don't repent or turn away from pride. Friends, pride has the potential to stop your destiny from marching forward. Why? That is because God hates it and resists the very people who walk in it. Remain humble before God and He will keep on elevating your life.

1 Peter 5:5-7

Likewise you younger people, submit yourselves to *your* elders. Yes, all of *you* be submissive to one another, and be clothed with humility, for "God resists the proud, But gives grace to the humble." Therefore humble yourselves under the mighty hand of God, that He may exalt you in due time, casting all your care upon Him, for He cares for you.

Saints, it doesn't matter where you live or your background. If only you can walk in humility to God, your life will never remain the same in Christ Jesus.

7 Scriptures About Pride

(1). Jeremiah 9:23-24

Thus says the Lord: "Let not the wise *man* glory in his wisdom, Let not the mighty *man* glory in his might, Nor let the rich *man* glory in his riches; But let him who glories glory in this, That he understands and knows Me, That I *am* the Lord, exercising lovingkindness, judgment, and righteousness in the earth. For in these I delight," says the Lord.

(2). Proverbs 29:23

A man's pride will bring him low, But the humble in spirit will retain honor.

(3). 1 John 2:16

For all that *is* in the world–the lust of the flesh, the lust of the eyes, and the pride of life–is not of the Father but is of the world.

(4). Isaiah 2:12

For the day of the Lord of hosts Shall come upon everything proud and lofty, Upon everything lifted up–And it shall be brought low.

(5). Proverbs 16:5

Everyone proud in heart *is* an abomination to the Lord; *Though they join* forces, none will go unpunished.

(6). Daniel 5:20

But when his heart was lifted up, and his spirit was hardened in pride, he was deposed from his kingly throne, and they took his glory from him.

(7). Proverbs 15:25

The Lord will destroy the house of the proud, But He will establish the boundary of the widow.

May you stay away from pride to avoid its consequences. God hates pride and resists the proud!

Kings Who Got Judged Because of Pride

(1). KING HEROD

There was a time when King Herod persecuted the Church of God. He killed James, the brother of John, with the sword and then arrested Peter and put him in prison. However, God judged him by sending an angel to afflict him with a serious sickness because of pride. Friends, pride will kill you before your time. Just be careful! Yes, at one time, Herod arrayed himself in royal apparel, sat on his throne and gave an oration and people likened him to the voice of God. He crossed the danger zone and God immediately judged him.

Acts 12:20-23

Now Herod had been very angry with the people of Tyre and Sidon; but they came to him with one accord, and having made Blastus the king's personal aide their friend, they asked for peace, because their country was supplied with food by the king's country. So on a set day Herod, arrayed in royal ap- parel, sat on his throne and gave an oration to them. And the people kept shouting, "The voice of a god and not of a man!" Then im- mediately an angel of the Lord struck him, because he did not give glory to God. And he was eaten by worms and died.

Sadly, King Herod died mysteriously! It was all because of pride that was at work in his life.

(2). King Nebuchadnezzar

King Nebuchadnezzar was another person whom God judged because of pride. He exalted himself by ascribing glory, majesty, strength, and honour to himself. It never took long for God to have judged him. In fact, the Bible says that while his words were in his mouth, a voice spoke from above and that was the end of his rulership over people. God punished Nebuchadnezzar because of his arrogance or excessive pride. The Almighty God drove him away from people into the wilderness and he ate grass like an ox.

Daniel 4:29-33

> At the end of the twelve months he was walking about the royal palace of Baby-

lon. The king spoke, saying, "Is not this great Babylon, that I have built for a royal dwelling by my mighty power and for the honor of my majesty?" While the word *was still* in the king's mouth, a voice fell from heaven: "King Nebuchadnezzar, to you it is spoken: the kingdom has departed from you! And they shall drive you from men, and your dwelling *shall be* with the beasts of the field. They shall make you eat grass like oxen; and seven times shall pass over you, until you know that the Most High rules in the kingdom of men, and gives it to whomever He chooses." That very hour the word was fulfilled concerning Nebuchadnezzar; he was driven from men and ate grass like oxen; his body was wet with the dew of heaven till his hair had grown like eagles' *feathers* and his nails like birds' *claws*.

No matter what happened to Nebuchadnezzar, after seven years, he came back to his senses. He learned a lesson that only God is the King of kings. After his repentance, God restored him to the human kingdom. God is Almighty!

Daniel 4:34-37

And at the end of the time I, Nebuchadnezzar, lifted my eyes to heaven, and my understanding returned to me; and I blessed the Most High and praised and honored Him who lives forever: For His dominion *is* an everlasting dominion, And His kingdom *is* from generation to generation. All the inhabitants of the earth *are* reputed as nothing; He does according to His will in the army of heaven And *among* the inhabitants of the earth. No one can restrain His hand Or say to Him, "What have You done?" At the same time my reason returned to me, and for the glory of my kingdom, my honor and splendor returned to me. My counselors and nobles resorted to me, I was restored to my kingdom, and excellent majesty was added to me. Now I, Nebuchadnezzar, praise and extol and honor the King of heaven, all of whose works *are* truth, and His ways justice. And those who walk in pride He is able to put down.

If you want to experience restoration in your life, humility is the way to go. Never entertain pride in your life, even for a second!

(3). King Uzziah

King Uzziah enjoyed brilliant success and power. That was until his pride sent him crashing down. Uzziah's fame, power and highly trained army didn't come from wishes. God himself gave Uzziah wonderful success as long as he sought the Lord. However, at some point, Uzziah lost sight of God as the true King and put himself on the throne. In pride, he saw himself as a ruler with the power to do whatever he wanted, even breaking God's law. God commanded only the priests to offer incense in the temple, but Uzziah, as king, no longer felt that God's rules applied to him. Sadly, God struck him with leprosy, and he died as a leper.

2 Chronicles 26:16-18 (AMP)

But when Uzziah became strong, he became so proud [of himself and his accomplishments] that he acted corruptly, and he was unfaithful *and* sinned against the Lord his God, for he went into the temple of the Lord to burn incense on the altar of incense. Then Azariah the priest went in after him, and with him eighty priests of the Lord, men of courage. They opposed King Uzziah and said to him, "It is not for you, Uzziah, to burn incense to the Lord, but for the priests, the sons of

Aaron who have been consecrated to burn incense. Get out of the sanctuary, for you have been unfaithful and will have no honor from the Lord God."

Remember this! *"Pride goes before destruction, and a haughty spirit before a fall."* (Proverbs 16:18). Saints, pride does not listen to divine counsel! Yes, King Uzziah never listened to the spiritual counsel that the priests gave him. Instead, he insisted on following his own ways. We have people today, even Christians, who can't take any advice or spiritual counsel. They want things to be done their own way. Then, others can't get corrected no matter how wrong they are. It was the same thing with King Uzziah. He did now want to buy into God's divine guidance. Sadly, he became a leper and died as a leper. God forbid!

2 Chronicles 26:16-19-21

Then Uzziah, with a censer in his hand to burn incense, was enraged; and while he was enraged with the priests, leprosy broke out on his forehead before the priests in the house of the Lord, beside the incense altar. As Azariah the chief priest and all the priests looked toward him, behold, he was leprous on his forehead; and they hurried him out of there, and he also hurried to get out because the Lord had stricken him. King Uzziah was a leper to the day of his death; and, being a leper, he lived in a separate house, for he was excluded from the house of the Lord. And his son Jotham took charge of the king's household, judging *and* governing the people of the land.

King Uzziah died a violent death! It was not God's will for him to have died like that.

Well, that is the destination of pride—it will kill you before your time. I don't think his death pleased God at all—He died prematurely! People of God never tread the way of pride. You will crush your own destiny in no time. Instead, keep on humbling yourself before God. Learn to take counsel and see other people better than yourself. The way of pride will cost you your entire life and destiny don't walk in it. If you want to find a special place in the heart of God, choose to walk in humility. I pray your spiritual eyes will open in Jesus' name.

Proverbs 16:25

There is a way which seems right to a man *and* appears straight before him, But its end is the way of death.

If you choose to walk in humility all the days of your life, your destiny will become unstoppable!!

CHAPTER SEVEN

Unrenewed Mind

Romans 12:1-2

I beseech you therefore, brethren, by the mercies of God, that you present your bodies a living sacrifice, holy, acceptable to God, *which is* your reasonable service. And do not be conformed to this world, but be transformed by the renewing of your mind, that you may prove what *is* that good and acceptable and perfect will of God.

Get it Renewed!

Your destiny has so many enemies that you need a vigilant spirit to fulfil it. Among all the enemies of your destiny, an unrenewed mind ranks top. When your mind is not renewed, just know that your entire life and destiny will come to a stop. Just be careful with what you allow in your mind and spirit. When your mind is not renewed, it means it is corrupted or polluted with the system of this world. It may also mean that it is not in alignment with the will of God in Christ Jesus. To be outside God's will as a child of God is an enormous risk, no matter which part of the world you live in. The will of God remains our greatest key to success.

Now, why do we need to renew our minds? Well, when God created Adam and Eve, their minds were God-aligned, driven, and intertwined. Then, after Adam sinned against God, his mind got corrupted and had no place in God's divine agenda. That is where it all started! However, when we get born again, we get to possess the mind of Christ Jesus. Sadly, for some people, even though they have the mind of Christ Jesus, they still incline their minds to the system of this corrupt world. Hence, the need for us to have our minds renewed with the Word of God. Only then can we walk in the will of God and fulfil our destinies in Christ Jesus.

Hebrews 4:12

For the word of God *is* living and powerful, and sharper than any two-edged sword, piercing even to the division of soul and spirit, and of joints and marrow, and is a discerner of the thoughts and intents of the heart.

James 1:21-22

Therefore lay aside all filthiness and overflow of wickedness, and receive with meekness the implanted word, which is able to save your souls. But be doers of the word, and not hearers only, deceiving yourselves.

It is vital as a child of God to walk in a renewed mind. Once your mind is not renewed with the Word of God, it will affect the growth of your faith. Just make sure that you don't allow the system of this world to pollute your mind. Any unrenewed mind is enmity to God. You can't please God when all that your mind thinks about is evil. Even your imagination must be in line with God's Word. Any negative thought in your life is proof that your mind needs to undergo a spiritual renewal by the Word of God. No matter your opinion, if your mind is not renewed, it will corrupt your destiny. Hence, never waste time to get it renewed in Jesus' name.

In the Old Testament, one reason God sent the flood to destroy people was because of an unrenewed mindset. The people's thoughts were evil constantly. Hence, they provoked God to anger and then He sent judgement. Anytime you think about evil, just know you are not pleasing to God. Even our Lord Jesus Christ said it in the Scriptures that whoever looks at a woman lustfully has committed adultery. Some people think the devil is the one responsible for their unrenewed minds. Well, that is a half-truth! Of course, he may get involved, but it is all up to you. Beloved, God destroyed the people because of their evil minds.

Genesis 6:5-8

Then the Lord saw that the wickedness of man *was* great in the earth, and *that* every intent of the thoughts of his heart *was* only evil continually. And the Lord was sorry that He had made man on the earth, and He was grieved in His heart. So the Lord said, "I will destroy

> man whom I have created from the face of the earth, both man and beast, creeping thing and birds of the air, for I am sorry that I have made them." But Noah found grace in the eyes of the Lord.

Friends, your spiritual soundness in Christ Jesus is very important to God. If you can guard the loins of your mind by feeding your mind with the Word of God, your life and destiny will be fruitful in no time. We are called to a life of greatness, witty inventions, and unusual accomplishments. Unfortunately, a corrupt mind will always hinder your life and destiny! Apart from that, a corrupt mind will expose you to satanic activities. Of course, no one is exempted from evil thoughts, but don't allow them into your life. If you do that, then it is your own choice! I pray your mind will get renewed with the Word of God in Jesus' name.

Ephesians 4:20-24

But you have not so learned Christ, if indeed you have heard Him and have been taught by Him, as the truth is in Jesus: that you put off, concerning your former conduct, the old man which grows corrupt according to the deceitful lusts, and be renewed in the spirit of your mind, and that you put on the new man which was created according to God, in true righteousness and holiness.

When you renew your mind with the Word of God, you will always scale heights of greatness in Christ Jesus.

Taking Authority

As a child of God, you have the authority to overcome negative thoughts in your life. Unfortunately, for some Christians, taking authority won't be that easy because they first need deliverance themselves. Besides, no matter your situation as a child of God, authority is your covenant right in Christ Jesus. Then, God's Word is the principal tool of deliverance and victory. Now, in case you are bound with oppressive thoughts, there is no way you can deliver yourself. You need someone that God has anointed with His power to deliver you. For example, God has anointed me to deliver people from all kinds of satanic oppression.

Many years ago, I had a spiritual vision in which I saw people dressed in white garments carrying loads on their bent backs. They looked weary, hopeless, defeated, and struggling in life. They were headed for a mountain I saw in that vision. At first, I did not understand what the vision was all about. Then, after a few days, one of my friends helped me to understand what it was. People of God, the vision I saw was a portion of Scripture in the book of Obadiah. The entire vision lasted for about 2 minutes. Without a doubt, visions are prophetic messages concerning God's divine plan or agenda for our lives in Christ Jesus.

Obadiah 1:17-18

But on Mount Zion there shall be deliverance, And there shall be holiness; The house of Jacob shall possess their possessions. The house of Jacob shall be a fire, And the house of Joseph a flame; But the house of Esau *shall be* stubble; They shall kindle them and devour them, And no survivor shall *remain* of the house of Esau," For the Lord has spoken.

During the same week as my vision, a friend of mine explained its meaning to me. He said that those dressed in white garments were children of God. Why?

That was because white garments in the Bible stand for the righteousness of the saints. Then, the people I saw carrying heavy loads on their backs were Christians whom the devil had enslaved. Further, in that vision, I heard God say to me: *These people have been enslaved never again should they be enslaved.* Saints, it was from there and then the anointing for deliverance came upon my life.

A few days later, when I prayed for people, I could see them getting delivered from all kinds of satanic oppressions. However, every child of God must learn how to take authority against all works of the devil by themselves. Jesus' blood has qualified you and me to walk in the authority of God. In case you have dirt and negative thoughts in your mind, all you need to do is take authority over them in the name of Jesus Christ. Nothing else! Most of the battles of the mind are spiritual, and they need spiritual authority to overcome them.

Many years ago, there was a time in my life when the devil was bombarding me with negative thoughts. However, to overcome them, I had to learn how to use the authority of God granted to us in Christ Jesus. Any child of God can take authority against evil thoughts or unclean spirits using the name of Jesus. Why? That is because Jesus Christ has given us divine power both in Heaven and on Earth to use. Why? That is because He wants us to walk in supernatural dominion and blessings. Nothing more and nothing less!!

Ephesians 6:10-13

Finally, my brethren, be strong in the Lord and in the power of His might. Put on the whole armor of God, that you may be able to stand against the wiles of the devil. For we do not wrestle against flesh and blood, but against principalities, against powers, against the rulers of the darkness of this age, against spiritual *hosts* of wickedness in the heavenly *places*. Therefore take up the whole armor of God, that you may be able to withstand in the evil day, and having done all, to stand.

The above Scripture enables us to understand that all the battles of life are spiritual. Hence, they demand a spiritual approach!!

2 Corinthians 10:1-5

Now I, Paul, myself am pleading with you by the meekness and gentleness of Christ– who in presence *am* lowly among you, but being absent am bold toward you. But I beg *you* that when I am present I may not be bold with that confidence by which I intend to be bold against some, who think of us as if we walked according to the flesh. For though we walk in the flesh, we do not war according to the flesh. For the weapons of our warfare *are* Not carnal but mighty in God for pulling down strongholds, casting down arguments and every high thing that exalts itself against the knowledge of God, bringing every thought into captivity to the obedience of Christ.

It doesn't matter your race, background, or even your age, you have the authority of God. You have the authority to stop evil thoughts in your life in Christ Jesus!!

Luke 10: 17-19

Then the seventy returned with joy, saying, "Lord, even the demons are subject to us in Your name." And He said to them, "I saw Satan fall like lightning from heaven. Behold, I give you the authority to trample on serpents and scorpions, and over all the power of the enemy, and nothing shall by any means hurt you.

Don't allow negative thinking to determine your life or future. Instead, overcome them by using the name of Jesus Christ by faith.

Spiritual Responsibility

One of my spiritual mentors once said that an irresponsible faith is not faith. What does that mean? Well, irresponsible faith is where you want God to do everything for you. For example, when Jesus commanded Lazarus to come forth out of the grave, he was still bound and clothed in grave clothes. Then, Jesus asked the people to remove all the ropes and grave clothes from him. He further said to people, *"Loose him, and let him go."* There are things God will do for us, and then there are also things we need to do with God's divine help. Some people are waiting for

God to take authority against the devil on their behalf.

Taking authority against the devil and his cohorts is our covenant responsibility, not God's responsibility! Many people are waiting for God to move when God is waiting for them to do so. Saints, you can't leave everything up to God. That is an irresponsible faith. Some people want God to pray and read the Bible for them—sorry, it doesn't work that way. God has already done everything we need today in the covenant of redemption, but all we need is to become responsible. Then other Christians are waiting for God to take negative thoughts away from them. Well, that won't happen—it is your duty or responsibility to do so.

Isaiah 54:17

No weapon formed against you shall prosper, And every tongue *which* rises against you in judgment You shall condemn. This *is* the heritage of the servants of the Lord, And their righteousness *is* from Me," Says the Lord.

In one of his books, Rev. Kenneth E. Hagin shared a story where Jesus came to him in a vision, and both were having a conversation. Then, there appeared in between them a creature like a monkey, a demonic figure that obstructed their conversation. However, the next thing Kenneth E. Hagin did was to take authority against it, and it fell to the ground instantly. In no time, Jesus and Hagin resumed their conversation. Now, out of curiosity, Hagin asked Jesus why He did not deal with that demon. Well, Jesus said to him He would not have done it! Why? That was because He had already given the Church authority and power over the devil.

When Christians understand the authority Jesus has given them, that will change many things in their lives. As long as you are born again, washed in the blood of Jesus, you need to exercise your authority against all negative thoughts. Perhaps some of you have done it, yet there are no results to match. Well, you need to grow in the knowledge and power of God. How? There is no other way to grow your authority and power in Christ Jesus, apart from God's Word, prayer, and fasting. Then, you also need to start from where you are! It is not something that happens overnight instead; you need to grow in it gradually.

For example, many years ago, there was a place I used to go for prayer. All I was doing in that place was praying and studying God's Word. Sometimes, I would be in that place for 3 hours or more, and rain would descend on me just like that. Then, one day, God spoke to me to go to a hospital in our city and pray for the sick. Without wasting time, I obeyed that divine instruction from God and went the following week. I'm glad to say that the nurses permitted me to pray for the sick. I remember ministering the Word of God and calling people to give their lives to Jesus Christ, and some did. However, it doesn't happen overnight!

Mark 16:20

And they went out and preached everywhere, the Lord working with *them* and confirming the word through the accompanying signs. Amen.

Most often, people are waiting for God when God is waiting for them. In the above Scripture, the disciples went first preaching God's Word and God worked with them. How? By confirming the Word of God, they preached with signs, miracles, and wonders.

Now, concerning my visit to the hospital mentioned earlier, people got healed and gave their lives to Jesus. Saints, when you act upon God's Word or instructions, something powerful happens. Hence, today I'm operating from a different realm of authority and power in Christ Jesus. Friends, stop waiting for God—He is waiting for you — get up and do something!!

Acts 19:11-12

Now God worked unusual miracles by the hands of Paul, so that even handkerchiefs or aprons were brought from his body to the sick, and the diseases left them and the evil spirits went out of them.

Miracles don't happen just because they have to. No! In the same way, your destiny won't just get fulfilled by itself, you need to take responsibility. If your destiny fails, it is not God's fault, but your fault. God has already done everything we need to fulfil our destinies in a grand style. Of course, it is our responsibility to ensure that we find the right tools to enhance the fulfilment of our destinies. Most often, we must deal with all the enemies of our destiny in Christ Jesus, otherwise, nothing will happen for us. Yes, don't wait for God! Instead, stand up in faith and fight against all the powers of darkness hindering your destiny.

Beloved, as we come to the end of this book, I would love you to understand that your destiny is glorious in Christ Jesus. All you need is to be a responsible person through the empowerment of the Holy Spirit. God bless you!!

Final Words of Faith

1. Growing up spiritually to overcome all the enemies of your destiny is your covenant responsibility in Christ Jesus.

2. Spiritual immaturity is an enormous risk. Never embrace it at all if you want to fulfil your destiny in a grand style.

3. The enemies of your destiny within, are more susceptible than the ones without. Just be careful!

4. Living to love God in your life is one of the greatest keys to overcoming the enemies of your destiny.

5. You don't fight against the enemies of your destiny, to make a point, but to obey the Word of God.

6. If you want to change the level of your life, you must first triumph over the enemies of your destiny in Christ Jesus.

7. The Holy Spirit is the architect behind the power we need to overcome all the enemies of our destiny. Without Him, all our efforts will be futile.

OTHER BOOKS BY GEORGE MFULA

- The Covenant Force of Righteousness
- Keys to Preserving Your Destiny
- Walking In Financial Dominion
- Unveiling the Hidden Treasures of Redemption
- The Broken & Forgotten Woman
- Understanding the Divine Secrets of God
- The Secret Place
- Nine Pillars of Success
- Winning the Battle Over Fear
- From Prison to Palace
- The Believer's Authority
- Plans, Purposes and Pursuits
- Breaking Satanic Limitations
- The Incredible Power of God's Word
- Following God's Plan for Your Life
- Exploits of Faith
- The Power of Prayer
- Dynamics of Bible Holiness

- The Holy Spirit, His Presence & Works
- Forgiveness
- Growing Up Spiritually
- The Power of the Blood
- The Power of Endurance
- The Mystery Behind God's Voice
- Divine Wisdom
- Divine Love
- Understanding the Anointing
- Divine Favour
- Divine Healing

MINISTRY CONTACT DETAILS

Email: rawc-sydney@homail.com

Phone: +61-425-338-781

For more information

please visit our website:

WWW.RISEANDWALK.ORG.AU

ABOUT THE AUTHOR

GEORGE MFULA is the overseer of Rise & Walk Church, Australia. He is an author, speaker, pastor, leader, teacher, and prophet. His mandate is to liberate people from all oppressions of the devil through the preaching and teaching of the Word of Faith. His passion is to glorify Jesus and declare him Lord to all nations of the earth through the matchless power of the pure Word of God and the Holy Spirit.

ABOUT THE BOOK

The enemies of your destiny are things that have the potential to stop God's divine purpose for your life. Often, people are always afraid of the enemies without, and not the enemies within. The enemies without are things out there, such as witches, powers of darkness, and cosmic powers. While the enemies within are the things we neglect to deal with in our personal lives. Many people, even Christians, spend most of their time blaming the devil in their lives. Of course, the devil is our greatest enemy of all time. However, Jesus has overcome Him for us on the cross. Hence, instead of focusing on the devil, let us focus on Jesus.

The enemies within are the very strongholds of the enemies without—the devil and his cohorts. However, the devil can't overcome you if only you can take charge of the enemies within. The enemies within include fear, ignorance, laziness, disobedience, unbelief, sin, pride, and much more to mention. Friends, we don't need to be ignorant of our authority over the devil in Christ Jesus. Let us move from spiritual blindness to spiritual enlightenment! You and I are born to dominate!

Get this book! You will scale greater heights of dominion over all the enemies of your soul and destiny in Christ Jesus. God bless you!!

www.ingramcontent.com/pod-product-compliance
Lightning Source LLC
Chambersburg PA
CBHW030221170426
43194CB00007BA/812